NONVERBAL COMMUNICATION

THE RANDOM HOUSE ENGLISH SERIES

NONVERBAL COMMUNICATION

by William Reynolds

RANDOM HOUSE SCHOOL DIVISION
Random House, Inc. New York

Material Developed in Association with PAIDEIA, INC.

contents

Unit 1
COMMUNICATION
PAGE 8

Unit 2
IMAGE
PAGE 14

Copyright © 1973 by Random House, Inc.

All rights reserved under International and Pan-American Copyright Conventions. Published in the United States by Random House, Inc., New York, and simultaneously in Canada by Random House of Canada Limited, Toronto.

Library of Congress Catalog Card Number: F2-3000
International Standard Book Number: 0-394-02719-1
Manufactured in the United States of America

The Author: William Reynolds, M.A., is a teacher of English and Chairman of the English Department at Bellport High School in Brookhaven, New York. In addition to *Nonverbal Communication,* Mr. Reynolds is the author of *Dialects in America, The Nature of Language* and *Affective Diction.*

Project Editor: Carl A. Barth
Assistant Editor: Ken Handel

Acknowledgements

For permission to use copyright material acknowledgement is made to the following:

Gene Byrnes for notes on cartooning technique. Copyright © 1950 by Gene Byrnes.

Condé Nast Publications, Inc. for diagram from *Vogue's Book of Etiquette and Good Manners.* Copyright © 1969 by Condé Nast Publications, Inc.

Consolidated Book Publishers for recipe from *The American Woman's Cookbook.* Copyright © 1950 by Processing and Books, Inc. and published by Culinary Arts Institute, Chicago. Reprinted by Permission of Consolidated Book Publishers.

Bob Dylan for excerpt from *Positively Fourth Street.* Copyright © by Bob Dylan.

Julius Fast for excerpt from *Body Language.* Copyright © 1970 by Julius Fast.

Edward T. Hall for excerpt from *The Silent Language.* Copyright © 1966 by Edward T. Hall. Reprinted by permission of Doubleday & Company, Inc.

Edward T. Hall and Mildred Hall for excerpts from "The Sounds of Silence." Copyright © 1971 by Edward and Mildred Hall.

The New Yorker for "The Unwritten." Copyright © 1971 by The New Yorker Magazine, Inc. Reprinted by permission.

Random House, Inc. for definition from *The Random House College Dictionary.* Copyright © 1972 by Random House, Inc. Reprinted by permission.

Random House, Inc. for excerpt from *Walden and Other Writings* by Henry David Thoreau.

The Saturday Evening Post for quote by Hal Chadwick. © 1971 by The Saturday Evening Post Company. Reprinted by permission.

Kitte Turmell for excerpt from "Kitte Turmell's Teenager," a syndicated newspaper column. Copyright © Kitte Turmell.

TIME, The Weekly Newsmagazine for excerpts on the Paris Conference. © 1968 by Time, Inc. Reprinted by permission.

Warm Music, for an excerpt from "The Storm," by Rod McKuen. Copyright © 1967 by Warm Music, from the Warner Bros. album, "The Sea."

Book Design by
Chestnut House/Norman Baugher

Unit 3
BODY ENGLISH
PAGE 24

Unit 4
SPACE, DISTANCE, and SILENCE
PAGE 46

Illustrations and Cartoons

Page 2. Cartoon by Capelini. Copyright © by the Ben Roth Agency.

Pages 4, 5, 8, 15, 24, 43, and 46. Cartoons by Thurber. Copyright © 1943 by James Thurber. Copyright © 1971 by Helen W. Thurber and Rosemary Thurber Sauers. From *Men, Women and Dogs*, published by Harcourt Brace Jovanovich, New York. Originally printed in *The New Yorker*.

Page 12. Cartoon by Emett. Copyright © by *Punch*, England.

Page 13. Drawing by Rube Goldberg. Copyright © by Rube Goldberg. Permission granted by King Features Syndicate.

Page 14. Cartoon by Lorenz. Copyright © 1966 by The Curtis Publishing Company. Reprinted by permission from *The Saturday Evening Post*.

Page 15. Cartoon by Richter. Copyright © 1968 by The New Yorker Magazine, Inc.

Page 16. Cartoon by Frascino. Copyright © 1971 by The New Yorker Magazine, Inc.

Page 17. Cartoon by Brammeier. Courtesy *Look* Magazine.

Page 18. Cartoon by Hageman. Copyright © 1971 by Saturday Review, Inc.

Page 21. Cartoon by Lorenz. Copyright © 1971 by The New Yorker Magazine, Inc.

Page 21. Cartoon by Reilly. Copyright © 1971 by The New Yorker Magazine, Inc. Copyright © by Ethel W. Webster.

Page 22. Drawing by Webster. Copyright © by Ethel W. Webster.

Page 23. Cartoon by Whitney Darrow, Jr. Copyright © 1968 by The New Yorker Magazine, Inc.

Page 26. Cartoon by Chas. Addams. Copyright © 1946 by The New Yorker Magazine, Inc.

Page 26. Cartoon by Chas. Addams. Copyright © 1950 by The New Yorker Magazine, Inc.

Page 26. Cartoon by Stan Hunt. Copyright © 1966 by Saturday Review, Inc.

Page 26. Cartoon by Berg. Copyright © by E. C. Publications, Inc.

Page 28. Cartoon by Reilly. Copyright © 1971 by The New Yorker Magazine, Inc.

Page 31. Drawings by Gene Byrnes. Copyright © 1950 by Gene Byrnes.

Page 31. Drawings of wolf facial expressions and tail positions. From *Behavior*, 1:81-129, in an article by Schenkel; translated from the German by Agnes Klasson. 1945. Copyright © E. J. Brill, Leiden, The Netherlands. Reprinted by permission.

Page 34. Cartoon by Boltinoff. Copyright © by the Ben Roth Agency.

Page 34. Cartoon by Carbi. Copyright © by *Carrefour*, France.

Page 35. Cartoon by Robert Day. Copyright © 1971 by The New Yorker Magazine, Inc.

Page 38. Cartoon by Canzler. Copyright © by the Ben Roth Agency.

Page 38. Cartoon by Aagaard. Copyright © 1955 by The Curtis Publishing Company. Reprinted by permission from *The Saturday Evening Post*.

Page 39. Cartoon by Faizant. Copyright © by Indéréa, France.

Page 40. Cartoon by Skaerbaek. Copyright © by P.I.B., Copenhagen, Denmark.

Page 40. Photograph. Copyright © Ken Regan.

Page 41. Cartoon by Yates. Copyright © 1955 by The Curtis Publishing Company. Reprinted by permission from *The Saturday Evening Post*.

Page 42. Cartoon by Faizant. Copyright © by Indéréa, France.

Page 42. Cartoon by Webster. Copyright © by the W.C.C. Publishing Company, Inc.

Page 44. Cartoon by Paul Peter Porges. Copyright © 1966 by Saturday Review, Inc.

Page 45. Cartoon by Jurg Spahr. Copyright © by Monsieur, Switzerland.

Page 47. Cartoon by Drucker. Copyright © 1971 by The New Yorker Magazine, Inc.

Page 49. Editorial cartoon by Hugh Haynie of the Louisville Courier-Journal. Copyright © by the Los Angeles Times Syndicate. Reprinted by permission.

Page 53. Cartoon by Censoni. Copyright © 1966 by Saturday Review, Inc.

Page 53. Cartoon by Martin. Copyright © 1971 by Saturday Review, Inc.

Page 55. Cartoon by Fisher. Copyright © 1971 by The New Yorker Magazine, Inc.

Page 58. Cartoon by Miller. Copyright © 1971 by The New Yorker Magazine, Inc.

Page 59. Cartoon by Chas. Addams. Copyright © by Chas. Addams.

Page 60. Cartoon by C.E.M. Copyright © 1967 by The New Yorker Magazine, Inc.

Page 61. Cartoon by Goldberg. Copyright © 1968 by Saturday Review, Inc.

Page 63. Cartoon by Cosper. Copyright © by Hudibras, Denmark.

Bob leaves his apartment at 8:15 A.M. and stops at the corner drugstore for breakfast. Before he can speak, the counterman says, "The usual?" Bob nods yes. While he savors his Danish, a fat man pushes onto the adjoining stool and overflows into his space. Bob scowls and the man pulls himself in as much as he can. Bob has sent two messages without speaking a syllable.

Henry has an appointment to meet Arthur at 11 o'clock; he arrives at 11:30. Their conversation is friendly, but Arthur retains a lingering hostility. Henry has unconsciously communicated that he doesn't think the appointment is very important or that Arthur is a person who needs to be treated with respect.

George is talking to Charley's wife at a party. Their conversation is entirely trivial, yet Charley glares at them suspiciously. Their physical proximity and the movements of their eyes reveal that they are powerfully attracted to each other.

José Ybarra and Sir Edmund Jones are at the same party and it is important for them to establish a cordial relationship for business reasons. Each is trying to be warm and friendly, yet they will part with mutual distrust and their business transaction will probably fall through. José, in Latin fashion, moved closer and closer to Sir Edmund as they spoke, and this movement was miscommunicated as pushiness to Sir Edmund, who kept backing away from this intimacy, and this was miscommunicated to José as coldness. The silent languages of Latin and English cultures are more difficult to learn than their spoken languages.

In each of these cases, we see the subtle power of nonverbal communication. The only language used throughout most of the history of humanity (in evolutionary terms, vocal communication is relatively recent), it is the first form of communication you learn. You use this preverbal language, consciously and unconsciously, every day to tell other people how you feel about yourself and them. This language includes your posture, gestures, facial expressions, costume, the way you walk, even your treatment of time and space and material things.

from "The Sounds of Silence"
by Edward and Mildred Hall

preface

There is more to human communication than meets the ear. Most of the "more" meets the eye. But some of it works through other senses, such as touch, or through other things that are related to the senses, such as space or distance. There is more to telling than talk.

This book asks you to examine some of the most common aspects of nonverbal communication or "body language." Sometimes body language completely takes the place of speech. At other times body language is used in addition to speech. In either case, its contribution to communication is important beyond words.

This is a book of activities, not a book of lectures. Each activity provides you and your classmates with just enough information to get you started on your own studies of nonverbal behavior. Most activities ask you and your classmates to serve as "subjects" for study. Other activities ask you to observe people outside class. From these activities, you will discover a great deal about yourself and your "style" of communicating wordlessly. You will also learn to "read" the body language of others. Such knowledge comes in handy. But keep in mind that your classmates are also learning to "read" at the same time! With that in mind. . .

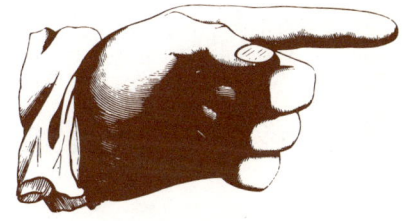

Unit 1
communication

1 Sometimes it seems that computers can be made to do almost anything. A recent newspaper item reported that a computer had been programmed to sing a popular song. What's more, a second computer had been programmed to accompany it on a piano! That was clearly a great achievement. But that achievement is quite simple compared with the task you and your classmates are going to try now: the programming of two "computers" to have a conversation. The topic of this computer conversation? **Peanut Butter and Jelly Sandwiches!** Here is what you do:

1. Choose one member of your class to serve as *Computer Expert*. It will be his job to direct the activity and to write a record of the computer conversation on the chalkboard.

2. The Computer Expert divides the class into two groups of about the same size. The groups sit apart from each other. Each group represents one of the "computers" about to converse with the other. The Computer Expert names one group *Computer A* and the other *Computer B*.

3. Next, the Computer Expert asks each member of both groups to write down *three different statements* that could come up in a conversation about peanut butter and jelly sandwiches.

4. Then, on another sheet of paper, which will be the computer print-out sheet, each member of both groups numbers a column from 1 to 20. Then he writes an *A* before each *odd* number and a *B* before each *even* number. The Computer Expert does the same thing on the chalkboard.

5. The two "computers" are now ready to converse. To get the conversation started, the Computer Expert asks one member of Computer A to read aloud any *one* of the three statements he wrote down. The Computer Expert records this sentence after A-1 on the chalkboard and each member of the class records this same statment after A-1 on his print-out sheet.

6. It is now Computer B's turn to respond to Computer A. Any member of Computer B who has a statement already prepared that will relate to or answer Computer A's statement volunteers to read his statement by raising his hand. The Computer Expert calls on one volunteer from Computer B who then reads his sentence. The Computer Expert records the statement on the chalkboard after the number B-2, and the class copies it onto their individual print-out sheets. The two computers take turns offering statements to the Computer Expert in this way until all twenty places on the print-out sheet are filled. The class then keeps its copies of the print-out sheet for use in the next activity. **NOTE:** *As far as is possible, each statement fed into the computers should have something to do with the statement made by the other computer immediately before it. No statements may be made up at the last minute. Each statement must be one that was written down before the start of the conversation.*

Nonverbal Communication

 Analyze the results of your computer conversation. Here is what you do:

1. One volunteer from Computer A and one from Computer B go to the front of the classroom. The two volunteers give an oral reading of the computer print-out sheet written during Activity 1. Each volunteer reads the statements which were made by his own computer.

2. Next, another volunteer from Computer A and another from Computer B go to the front of the classroom. They talk "off-the-cuff" for a minute or so on the same topic used in the computer conversation—peanut butter and jelly sandwiches. You and your classmates should pay close attention to their performance. Make mental notes of any general difference between this conversation and the one held by the two computers.

3. The class then compares the oral reading with the off-the-cuff conversation. For example, what features of normal conversation were missing from the computer chat but were present in the off-the-cuff conversation? Do you think it possible to program a computer conversation to *include* these features? This question assumes, of course, that such features are important to communication. *Are* they important? What makes you think so?

Now that you have dabbled in electronics, electricity should be a snap for you. The diagram shown on the facing page is similar to a drawing of an electrical circuit. The circuit in this case is the circuit of human communication. The diagram shows, in a simplified way, what happens when two people are involved in conversation. Study the diagram until you understand its lines and labels.

The diagram seems to suggest a very tidy situation. One person translates a concept into his own words and has his say while the other person listens. The listener hears the words, translates the words back into a concept, mulls it all over, and then has *his* say. This process continues back and forth. It is hard to imagine anything simpler. Why is it, then, that the communication circuit so often blows a fuse and has a short-circuit breakdown? Even though a speaker's voice is doing its job and his listener's ears are in good working order, breakdowns do occur in communication. In discussion with your classmates, make a list of some of the factors that cause short circuits in communication between two people. Save the list to use later on.

4. Discuss with your classmates each of the following conversational situations. What short circuits might be expected to occur in the communication circuit of each? Add any new short-circuit factors to your present list.

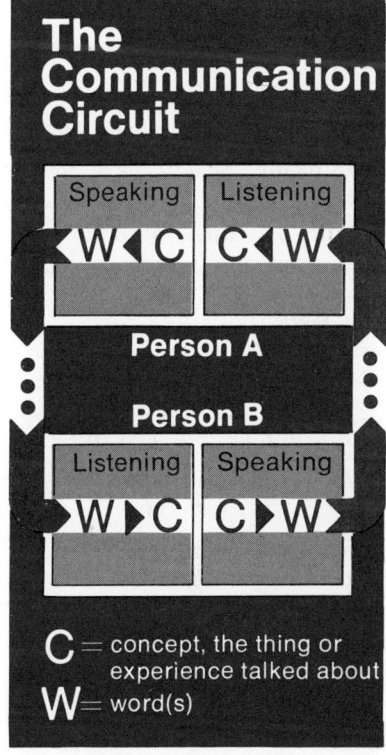

	PERSON A	PERSON B
Situation 1	Doesn't know B.	Doesn't know A.
Situation 2	Is very interested in baseball and supposes that B is, too. This person is a girl.	Has no interest in baseball. This person is a boy.
Situation 3	Thinks he's an expert on a subject, but he is really far from being an expert.	Is impressed by A's great grasp of the subject and wants to learn from A.
Situation 4	Thinks he's an expert on a subject and feels that B knows nothing about the subject.	Is really an expert on the subject.
Situation 5	Has just come home from a difficult day at the office; wants to relax and read the evening newspaper.	A's wife; wants to talk with A about a serious matter.
Situation 6	Is highly educated, with more degrees than a thermometer; likes to impress people with this fact.	Quit school at age 16; is now a prizefighter.
Situation 7	Set up a few situations of your own that you are sure would cause some short circuits in communication.	

Nonverbal Communication 11

5 Pair up with one of your classmates. Working together, make up a one-minute conversation that shows some short circuit in communication. Present your conversation in front of your classmates. Then see if they can guess from your demonstration which communication short circuit you have shown. If you and your partner wish, you may use one of the situations listed in Activity 4. In your acting and conversing, try to behave free of exaggeration that would make guessing too easy for your classmates.

6 Write a short paper describing a situation from your own experience in which a communication short circuit occurred. Was the short circuit so bad that communication was a total failure? Or did you somehow manage to get the circuit back to working order? Perhaps you saw the difficulty coming and tried to adjust to it ahead of time. If so, what adjustments did you make? If not, what would you do if a similar situation happened again? This activity will prove especially interesting and humorous if you choose a communication situation in which the other party is a present member of your class. Persuade that classmate to write about the same situation. Then, in oral readings, compare your short-circuit experiences with those described by your classmates in their papers. If you and a classmate have written about the same experience, be sure to read the papers one after the other.

7 Now that you are an expert on some of the short circuits that can damage communication, draw a diagram that represents your idea of what the communication circuit is really like. Look again at the formal diagram on page 11. Then examine the two illustrations on pages 12 and 13. Use either the formal diagram or one of the illustrations as a model in drawing your idea of the human communication circuit. Display the finished product on the classroom bulletin board.

EMETT, ©PUNCH, ENGLAND

How To Make A Sedan Bigger Inside Without Making It Bigger Outside

When man (**A**) discovers the lack of trunk space in his new sedan, he gets hot under the collar and sparks (**B**) ignite fuse (**C**) setting off cannon (**D**) which shoots out cannonball (**E**) causing string (**F**) to open front hood (**G**) thus releasing football shoe (**H**) which boots out engine (**I**) and thereby creates a trunk in front.

Engine (**I**) flies end over end over car into baseball glove (**J**) and rebound of spring (**K**) causes glove (**J**) to toss engine (**I**) back into car above rear drive wheels where added weight causes string (**L**) to pull brace (**M**) from beneath shelf (**N**) dropping weight (**O**) which in turn causes wire (**P**) to pull up giant suction cups (**Q**) thereby raising the rear roofline, squaring it off, and creating additional space.

As rear roofline rises, it strikes bellows (**R**) and pressure of air blows whistle (**S**). Trained circus mouse (**T**), in trunk, hearing whistle thinks lunch is over and bulldozes his way towards front of car. During the process, he flattens rear seat (**U**) and thereby gives man A's sedan over twice the carrying space of any other sedan.

Should you face the same problem, but find a shortage of circus mice trained in the operation of bulldozers, all is not lost.

There already exists a sedan with a front trunk, square back, fold-down rear seat, and over twice the carrying space of any other sedan. (Oddly enough, it's called the Volkswagen Squareback Sedan.)

Simply see car dealer (**VW**).

Nonverbal Communication

IMAGE

Unit 2

Study the three cartoons at the bottom of pages 14, 15, and 16. Then decide which one of the definitions of *image* on page 16 is behind the humor in each cartoon. When you have done this, discuss the cartoons one by one. You can use the following suggestions to get you started.

Cartoon 1: Pretend you are Cauldwell. Describe a situation from your own experience when you found yourself in conversation with someone. His image in *your* mind was quite a bit different from his image in *his* own mind. In what ways did this difference affect communication between the two of you? If you were to draw a cartoon showing the situation, what changes would you make in the drawing of Cauldwell's conversation "partner"?

THE SATURDAY EVENING POST

"The truth is, Cauldwell, we never see ourselves as others see us."

14 Nonverbal Communication

"*A general! Goodness gracious, you don't look like a general!*"

Cartoon 2: The images we have of certain types of people are often nothing more than set ideas in our minds—ideas that frequently are not true when we finally meet such people face-to-face. What set ideas about images do you have? To help you find out, you might substitute *minister* or *politician* for *general* in the caption of the cartoon. Discuss each substitution with your classmates and describe in some detail the usual image of the person involved. If possible, describe situations from your own experience in which your preconceived image of a person was not accurate when you met him. Where do you suppose such set ideas about image come from? In what ways do they affect human communication?

Nonverbal Communication

im•age (im′ij), *n., v.* **-aged, -ag•ing.—***n.* **1.** a physical likeness or representation of a person, animal, or thing, photographed, painted, sculptured, or otherwise produced. **2.** an optical counterpart or appearance of an object, such as is produced by reflection from a mirror. **3.** a mental representation; idea; conception. **4.** form; appearance; semblance: *God created man in his own image.* **5.** counterpart; copy: *That child is the image of his mother.* **6.** a symbol; emblem. **7.** a type; embodiment: *He was the image of frustration.* **8.** a description of something in speech or writing. **9.** an idol or representation of a deity. **10.** *Rhet.,* a figure of speech, esp. a metaphor or a simile.

from *The Random House Dictionary of the English Language, College Edition.*

1

Cartoon 3: This cartoon touches on *two* of the definitions of *image* found in the dictionary entry. You have already discussed one of the two definitions while examining the *other* cartoons. What other definition is at work in the humor of cartoon 3? Do you know anyone, including yourself, whose idea of his own image seems based entirely on the sort of situation described in this other definition of *image*? If so, describe to your classmates how such an image can affect a person's communication with others.

2

3

"Wow!"

9 The word *person* comes from the Latin word *persona*, meaning "actor's mask" or "character in a play." How well do you think our use of *a person* reflects the Latin meanings? The cartoon of the author autographing his book is a good picture of the Latin meanings. Why? What does his behavior have to do with image? Draw a similar cartoon showing yourself in one of the daily masks you put on to suit a particular situation.

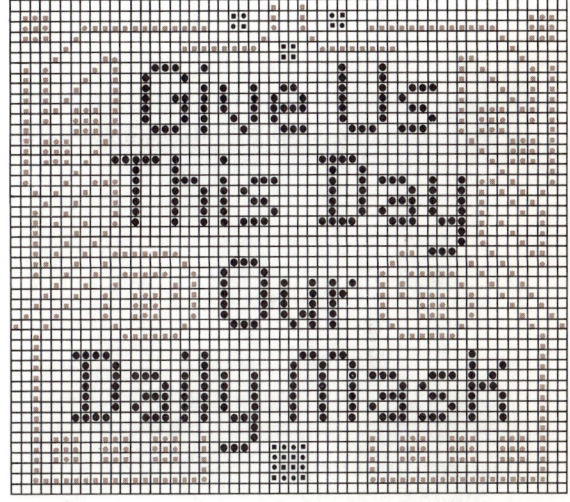

Nonverbal Communication

SR/MARCH 20, 1971

President Johnson's reaction to the Hurd painting might reasonably be called a human one. Why? If you don't think so, or even if you do, try this experiment. Persuade one of your classmates to bring to school an instant camera—one that takes and develops photographs in a minute or so. Have him photograph three or four of the class members. Then notice the reactions of each one when he sees the finished product. You might next try a similar experiment. Bring to school *two* recent photographs of yourself. One of the photos should be one that you think is a good likeness, true to your own ideas of what you look like; the other should be a poor likeness, at least from your point of view. Exchange photo sets with some of your classmates. Let your classmates guess which photo you prefer and which you dislike.

10 President Lyndon Johnson asked Norman Rockwell to paint his portrait. Mr. Rockwell tells the following anecdote about the experience:

HOW MIGHT MR. ROCKWELL ANSWER?

18 Nonverbal Communication

11 Pair up with a classmate and try the following experiment. Write an "image recipe" of (1) yourself, as you think you appear to your partner, and (2) your partner, as he appears to you. Your partner will be doing the same exercise from his point of view. The quickest way to arrive at the two recipes is to follow these steps. (1) Write down at least six adjectives that you feel describe your own image. (2) Write six that describe your partner's image. (3) Change each adjective on both lists into a noun. (4) Assign to *each* noun on both lists a specific quantity and measure, such as *4 pounds of conceit* or *a pinch of humility* or *3 tablespoons of humor*. Keep in mind that the relative amounts assigned to each item define your images just as clearly as do the nouns themselves. When you and your partner have completed your recipes, exchange and compare them. The most interesting comparison, of course, will be the one between your own recipe for yourself and the recipe for you made up by your partner. Keep the recipes for use in the next activity.

RED FLANNEL HASH

9 cooked beets, chopped
6 cooked potatoes, chopped
1 1/2 cups chopped cooked corned beef
1/2 cup fat, melted
2 teaspoons salt
1/8 teaspoon pepper
6 tablespoons water

Combine beets, potatoes, corned beef, fat, salt, pepper and water. Place in greased baking dish and bake in moderate oven (3506 F.) about 3/4 hour. Serves 6.

from *The American Woman's Cookbook*

---

12 Mark each of your two image recipes with the name of the person described. Then, together with your classmates, place your recipes in a loose pile on a table or desk at the front of the room. When all recipes have been gathered, follow these steps:

1. Two students each draw one recipe from the pile.

2. Each student reads aloud the recipe he has drawn, but does *not* reveal the name of the person described by it.

3. The class then discusses how well or how poorly the two persons described would probably get along together in an ordinary communication situation.

4. The class tries to guess which two persons are described in the recipes. No more than three guesses are allowed. If the class guesses who a person is, the person must tell whether he wrote the recipe himself or whether his partner wrote it. If the class does not guess, then the persons who read the recipes reveal who is being described in each.

5. Place used recipes aside and repeat the process with two new recipe readers.

Nonverbal Communication

13 Look again at the Cauldwell cartoon on page 14. Then read the lyric by Bob Dylan that appears here. Suppose that the cartoon's caption were erased and that Cauldwell were doing the talking. Would Dylan's words make any sense as a new caption for the drawing? Explain your answer. Write a short paper describing some time in your own life when you wished another person could see himself as you were seeing him. When the papers are finished, some of them should be read aloud. Compare your own experience with those described by your classmates in their papers.

I wish that for just one time
You could stand inside my shoes
And just for that one moment
I could be you.
Yes, I wish that for just one time
You could stand inside my shoes.
You'd know what a drag it is
To see you.

Bob Dylan

---

14 This lyric by Rod McKuen has a topic a lot like the Dylan lyric above. But McKuen wants a vantage point different from the one Dylan hopes for. What is the difference? Discuss it with your classmates. Then pretend that you are able to do what McKuen would like to do. Choose some person whose friendship is important to you, but who is not yet your friend. The person need not be a classmate or even someone your own age. You may choose anyone in your life. Write a short paper that describes what you think you would see if you were to look at yourself through the other person's eyes. In the last paragraph of the paper, try to state how you might change your image to bring about the friendship you desire. Give your finished paper to your teacher.

I love you, but I'm not always sure of
  what you are
And how you feel.
I'd like to crawl behind your eyes and see me
  the way you do.
Or climb through your mouth and sit on every
  word that
Comes up your throat.
Maybe I could be sure then.
Maybe I could know it as it is.

Rod McKuen

15 Each of the two cartoons on this page comments on one of the "gaps" so much in the news in recent years. One cartoon names one of the gaps. See if you can name the gap represented by the other cartoon. Discuss with your classmates the role played by image in the creation of both gaps.

"Say, Pop, is it really true that he never opened a credibility gap?"

"It so happens, Son, that the New York Supreme Court has recently ruled that a father is under no obligation to support an offspring who insists on a life style repugnant to the parent."

Nonverbal Communication 21

THE TIMID SOUL

Casper Milquetoast, the fellow addressing the snowman in the cartoon on this page, has apparently decided to change his doormat image. This suggests that a person can control his image almost at will. And if he can't do it by himself, then others can help him. Image-making is one of the services offered by public relations firms. The caption and cartoon shown on page 23 give a fair idea of how the public relations business operates. In the cartoon, a man from a firm is trying to sell his services to a senator. The cartoonist's choice of a subject is a good one. Political figures hardly ever enter a campaign without securing the services of a public relations firm. The firm's purpose is to make sure that the client's image appeals to the widest possible range of voters. Show business personalities often use public relations firms. In fact, the very term *personalities* suggests that image is particularly important to those in the entertainment world.

See if you have what it takes to be a successful public relations man or woman. Choose one of the following as your client: (1) a present-day political figure, (2) an entertainer, or (3) some other well-known person whose image you think needs improving. Then write a paper, addressed to your client, that gives your suggestions for improving his image. Be sure to point out early in the paper what you consider wrong about your client's present image. That way, your suggestions can be read in terms of the problems they are meant to solve. All through the paper, try to draw on everything you have learned about image from previous activities. If your teacher thinks it a good idea, you might mail your paper to the person you wrote about. But, since your client did not request the report, you'd better not send him a bill!

"With a good public-relations team on the job, Senator, you'll come through as a smart guy who happens to be inarticulate, instead of a guy who doesn't know what the hell he's talking about."

BODY ENGLISH

Unit 3

24 Nonverbal Communication

> **People convey feelings 7% because of the words actually said, 38% through tone of voice, 55% through expressions and posture.**
>
> —Dr. Albert Maehrabian

17 Look at the three cartoons and the comic strip on the next page. Then compare each of the four items against the "message equation" in the box above. The equation tells what features combine to make a typical emotional message. Note that the equation shows different percentages for each of the three features listed. This equation is not meant to be true of all emotional messages. But it is useful for general purposes at least. According to the equation, which feature is *most important* in an emotional message? Which feature is *least important*? And which feature has *in-between importance,* neither most nor least? To what extent do you agree with these rankings?

The characters in the cartoons and the comic strip are all sending an emotional message of one sort or another. And it happens that some of the characters are also receiving an emotional message at the same time. But concentrate only on the messages being sent. Assume that you are a "fly on the wall" in each situation shown. Take each cartoon one at a time and discuss with your classmates how faithfully the emotional messages of its characters reflect the percentages given in the equation. If necessary, rewrite the equation to describe any emotional message that seems to you in need of a new equation with different percentages.

Nonverbal Communication 25

TOTAL IMPACT OF AN EMOTIONAL MESSAGE = 7% words + 38% tone of voice + 55% facial expression and physical gestures.

"No wonder you're tired, poor dear, making all those mountains out of all those molehills all day."

26 Nonverbal Communication

18 Look again at the captioned cartoon and at the comic strip from the previous activity. The words in the cartoon's caption and in the comic strip balloons could be read aloud in tones of voice quite different from the tones the cartoonist was thinking of in each case. Try some different readings. First, read the caption of the cartoon the way you feel the cartoonist would read it. Explain why you chose that way. Then read the caption in a different way, but one that could still make sense in the situation shown. Explain your new reading to the class. Repeat the same process with the words of the comic strip. This will be more fun if a boy and girl read the dialogue together. When you have tried various readings of both items, discuss the readings with your classmates. How closely did each of the new readings match the drawings? Did the new readings seem to "go with" the facial expressions, gestures, space between characters, and other nonverbal features seen in the drawings? Give as many details as you can in stating your view.

19 **For the Boys:** Find a photograph, painting, or drawing (or do a drawing yourself) that illustrates the quotation from Shakespeare. In place of the italicized word, *wanton*, in the second line of the quotation, supply an adjective of your own choice. Choose one that suits the illustration you have chosen. Paste the illustration on a piece of paper. Then, under the illustration, copy the quotation as rewritten with your own adjective. On a *second* piece of paper, write a brief description of what you think the person in the illustration is saying with "her eye, her cheek, her lip, her foot."

For the Girls: Do as the boys are doing—only substitute *his* for *her* throughout the quotation.

For Everyone: Each group chooses four illustrated quotations from among those submitted by its members. Place the four papers on a table or desk near the front of the classroom. Use different tables for the papers of each group. In a second pile next to each pile of illustrated quotations, place the four descriptions that were written by the contributors. When this has been done, choose one classmate to go to the front of the room. This person selects, first, one illustrated quotation from the pile *not* submitted by his or her own group. Then he or she tries to guess which of the descriptions in the second pile was written to go with the selected quotation. As quotations and descriptions are used up, discard them. Repeat the process two more times with materials from each group. Use a different student selector each time. The activity is over when only one pair of items is left on each table.

◂ There's language in her eye, her cheek, her lip, Nay, her foot speaks; her *wanton* spirits look out At every joint and motive of her body.

from TROILUS AND CRESSIDA *by* Shakespeare

Nonverbal Communication 27

20 The adjectives listed in the box are often used by writers to describe the nonverbal messages "spoken" by eyes. Let's see now how well you and your classmates communicate with your eyes. Divide the class into groups of five or six members. Each group should contain both boys and girls. The members of each group, one at a time, choose one adjective from the list. The choice must be a secret to the other members. Then each member, in turn, uses his eyes to "send" to the other members the message suggested by the chosen adjective. The task for the viewers is to guess which adjective on the list is being communicated. While a member is trying to send his eye-message, he must cover the rest of his face (nose and mouth) with a piece of paper, so that only the eyes show. If, on the first try, no one guesses the correct adjective, the paper is lowered so that the nose shows too. If members still cannot come up with the correct adjective, the paper is taken away completely, so that the full face is revealed. Keep an accurate record of when each adjective was guessed and of the person who used it. When each group has completed the activity, the entire class compares results. The winners are those who were able to communicate successfully on their *first* try, with only the eyes exposed. Save all of your record sheets for use with the next activity.

21 Write the following four headings on the chalkboard: GUESSED ON FIRST TRY; GUESSED ON SECOND TRY; GUESSED ON THIRD TRY; NOT GUESSED. Use your records from the previous activity to list under the right heading each adjective used in the activity. The best way to do this is to read the adjectives on the list in order. Ask each group to report when one of its adjectives is read. When all used adjectives have been recorded in this way, discuss what seems to be their relative "sendability" by the eyes alone.

22 Divide the class into two groups of about equal size. The members of one group are dentists. The members of the other group are nose specialists. Each of the dentists draws one mouth on a small piece of paper. Each of the nose specialists draws a nose. All drawings should be front views, not profiles. When both groups have finished drawing, one member from each group collects his group's drawings and places them in a pile on a table or desk at the front of the classroom. The two piles must be kept separate. Three members of the class then go to the front of the room. Each takes, at random, one drawing from *each* of the two piles. The three artists next go to the chalkboard, where each draws a large oval face and copies onto it the mouth and the nose he selected from the two piles. The copies should be as faithful as possible. When the copying is complete, the three artists return to their seats. Now the trick is for you and your classmates to add a pair of eyes to each of the three faces. Choose from the collection of eyes in the cartoon. The eyes chosen for each face should be the pair that best completes the expression suggested by the mouth and nose already there. Complete one face at a time. When the class agrees on a pair of eyes for a face, one member of the class should go to the board and copy that pair onto the face. Then he adds eyebrows, ears, and hair of his own design. When all three of the faces are finished, discuss with your classmates possible verbal statements that might serve as captions to each drawing.

Nonverbal Communication

23

It has been said that "for Americans, eye behavior does duty as a kind of conversational traffic signal, to control how talking time is shared." Let's see what that statement means. Three conversational "traffic signals" are being used in the passage on the left below. Each of the three is indicated by a number preceding the signal. Match each signal with its meaning from among the four meanings listed on the right below. When you are sure of each match, go on to the next part of the activity.

Assume that you are a filmwriter trying to make a story into a movie script. You have decided to use the words of any conversation just as they appear in the story. But you wish to add acting directions to the conversation, so that the actors will know what to do with their eyes when speaking. In short, you want to provide conversational traffic signals. In your school literature book find a story that contains a conversation between two people and write such a script. Try to choose a conversation in which there is at least one fairly long bit of talking by one of the two characters. Copy the conversation from your book. Wherever you consider eye directions to be necessary, write such directions in parentheses *before* the part of the conversation to which each applies. Things such as (LOOK AWAY FROM LISTENER) or (GIVE LISTENER LONG LOOK) are the sorts of directions you should write. Save your script for possible use in the next activity.

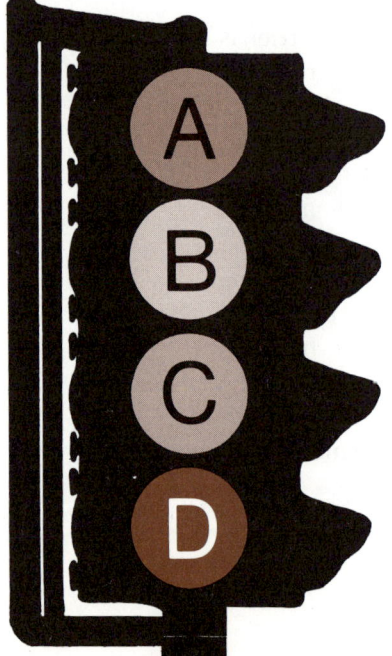

Joan and Sandra meet on the sidewalk. Greetings over with, Joan begins to talk. **(1)** She starts by looking to the right away from Sandra. **(2)** As she gets her conversation moving, she looks back at her friend from time to time at the end of a phrase or sentence. She does not look at her during hesitations or pauses, but only at natural breaks in the flow of her talk. **(3)** At the end, she gives Sandra a longer glance.

A. Speaker wants the listener to interrupt.

B. Speaker checks to see if the listener is paying attention and, in effect, is "asking" permission to continue talking.

C. Speaker is "telling" the listener that she is done talking.

D. Speaker is signaling that she wants time to organize what she is going to say and that she doesn't want to be distracted.

24 Make a second copy of the movie script you wrote during the previous activity. Then invite a classmate to join you in memorizing the script to act out before the class. The memorizing is necessary because both of you will need your eyes during the performance. Following your presentation, ask your classmates to comment on your selection of eye signals. Did your signals seem to suit the conversation? Be prepared to perform the drama (or a part of it) a second time, perhaps a little more slowly and with some exaggeration. Your audience may need a replay of signals missed, or poorly sent, the first time around.

All changes of expression are centered in the mouth, the eyes, and eyebrows—these are the only features that move of themselves. The eyes and the mouth are studied ceaselessly by the cartoonist who wishes to develop facility in facial expressions.

Gene Byrnes, Cartoonist

25 Man is not the only animal who communicates in body language. Most lower animals depend on body language far more than man does. The pictures here show some of the facial expressions and tail signals of the wolf. Study the pictures and try to decide what emotion each individual face or tail position is showing. Then, if you have a pet animal at home, make a record of his range of emotions in a series of drawings. Bring your sketches to class and display them on the bulletin board. For the time being, discuss with your classmates possible comparisons between man's body language and that of the lower animals.

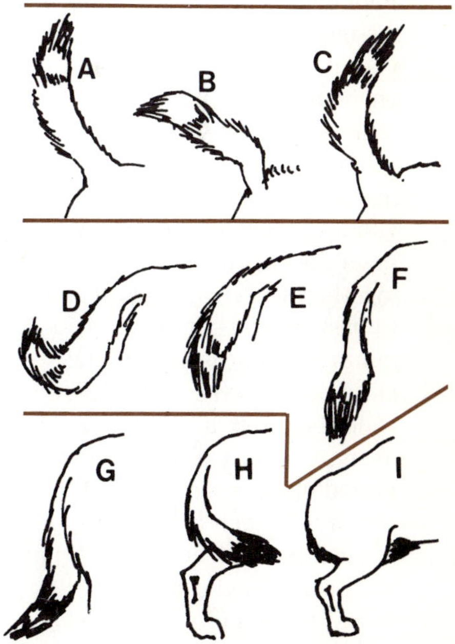

Nonverbal Communication 31

26 You might enjoy working alone or with others to create a "mood" collage. To a board about 18 by 24 inches attach pictures, drawings, or photographs of human faces expressing nonverbal messages of a *single mood*—for example, joy, sadness, anger, ecstasy, frustration, or any other mood you wish. The pictures used in the collage can be either obvious or subtle expressions of the mood selected. If you prefer, you may create two collages, one using mouths only, the other using just eyes. The collages may represent the same mood or two different moods. If you and your teacher choose to have the entire class work together, you might find it fun to post several smaller mounting boards around the classroom. Each smaller board should express a different mood. You and your classmates, over a period of days, can then add pictures to each collage until all are complete. Keep in mind that each completed collage must be an expression of a *single mood*.

27 Facial expressions change almost automatically to suit the message of a true statement. Speakers and listeners do not have to manufacture facial expressions when the communication is sincere and spontaneous. The expressions just happen. But what about those times when the speaker does not mean what he is saying, or when the listener's reaction is an artificial one that hides his true feelings? Unfortunately, such situations are common. For example, a girl might say to her rival: "My, Alice, what a perfectly gorgeous dress you're wearing!" You can imagine what the girl is really thinking, and you can picture, too, the facial expression accompanying her words. Other examples are easy to come up with. See what you and your classmates can think of. Taking turns, each of you demonstrates for the class an example of a communication situation in which facial expression and statement hide a speaker's real feelings. First, each performer speaks the statement and supports it with the appropriate facial expression. Then the class tries to guess the sort of situation in which such a statement and facial expression might appear. When everyone has had a chance to give an example, discuss with your classmates the effect of such examples on the communication circuit.

28 Of course, not all situations involving a false face and statement are bad or deceitful. Sometimes it is good not to reveal true feelings to a conversational partner. Most of these instances occur out of courtesy and respect for the partner's feelings. See if you and your classmates can think of some examples of this sort of situation. Describe each situation and explain why a false face and statement are good things in the context of the situation described.

ENOUGH OF FACES: IT'S TIME NOW TO CONSIDER *GESTURES*.

Nonverbal Communication

29 Gestures of the hands and arms are often used in place of verbal communication. Such gestures, without words, are most often used when verbal communication is *not practical, not necessary,* or *not desirable.* Each of these three categories is represented by one of the cartoons above. Match the cartoon and the category in each case. Then list the three categories on a sheet of paper and make a short list of similar gesturing situations under each heading. Save your list for the next activity.

30 Work with a classmate and compare the lists you made during the previous activity. Choose one situation from each of the three categories; then, without words, act out the three selections for the class. Ask your classmates (1) to guess the situation you are portraying in each instance, and (2) to decide whether gestures are used because words are *not practical, not necessary,* or *not desirable* in each situation shown. The gestures used in the skits should be formal gestures. These are gestures whose meanings are so widely known that the gestures convey the same message every time they are used.

31 Many gestures, perhaps most, are *informal*. These are gestures "made up" for a particular situation to meet a special need. Such gestures do not have the universal meaning of formal gestures. For example, many movie Westerns include a scene of a cavalry officer trying to make himself understood to a renegade Indian chief. The chief, in turn, is trying to make *his* needs known to the officer. Because neither one speaks the other's language, both must rely entirely on gestures for communicating. Even so (just to keep the movie audience tuned in to the situation), the officer and the Indian *do* speak while they perform their gestures! Of course, such situations probably never happened quite that way. But let's pretend, anyway, that they did. Pair up with a classmate. Each of the situations described to the right and on the next page involves two persons. You play the part of one person; your partner plays the other person. Select one of the situations to act out before the class. Pretend that neither of you can speak the other's language. However, just as in the movies, each of you should add speech to your gestures. That way your classmates will know what is going on. As in the game of charades, try to use gestures that are as close as possible to what the words mean. Don't be afraid to overact, or exaggerate.

Situation 1: A cavalry officer wants an Indian chief to give him a drink of water. The chief, however, is thirsty himself. His spring has run dry. Besides, he sees that the officer is wearing a canteen, and he thinks that the officer is holding out on him.

Situation 2: A beautiful native girl lives on an island where there are many more females than males. One day she happens to find a shipwrecked sailor. She wants him to come back with her to her father's hut so they can be married. The sailor doesn't want to go with her. On the other hand, he doesn't want to insult her either. 👉

"Let me do the palavering. My tongue is more forked than yours."

Nonverbal Communication 35

Situation 3: A foreign visitor to the United States approaches a policeman who is directing traffic. The visitor wants the policeman to explain the game of baseball to him. The policeman tries to do so.

Situation 4: An American girl on an African safari meets a native girl out in the bush country. The native girl likes the pith helmet that the American girl is wearing and wants to trade her necklace for it. The American understands after a while, agrees to the trade, but then wants her helmet back when she finds out that the necklace is made of lizards' ear lobes.

Situation 5: A situation that you make up yourself. Describe the situation to the class before performing it.

32 Now experiment with some gestures that *go with* speech and give it fuller meaning. Each member of the class, without telling his choice, selects one of the statements from the list below for expression, first, *by gesture only* . Taking turns, each member of the class stands and gives a *silent* demonstration of the gesture he thinks goes with the statement he has chosen. The other members have no more than three tries to guess which statement from the list is being demonstrated. After a correct guess, the performing student repeats the original gesture. But this time he speaks the statement that goes with it. After each wrong guess, the person who made the error must perform the gesture along with the statement *he* thought went with the gesture. Following three wrong guesses, the original performer combines the gesture and his chosen statement. Discuss any performance in which gesture and statement do not seem matched. Be prepared to defend any guess called "wrong" by the performer, but which seems "right" to you, given the gestures he made. A class vote is a good way to settle such differences of opinion.

1. "You bum—you struck out with the bases loaded!"
2. "I'm worried."
3. "Look, you can trust me."
4. "Listen, do you want it or not?"
5. "How was I to know?"
6. "Wow! A Rosecrested Bugnibbler!"
7. "Speak up. I can't hear you."
8. "Eeek! A mouse!"
9. "I accept the nomination."
10. "Get out and stay out."
11. "Everything is A-Okay."
12. "Have a seat."
13. "Peace."
14. "Two away out there, you guys!"
15. "The fish was *this* big."
16. "Nancy, this is Melvin. Melvin, Nancy."
17. "Aw, g'wan. You're putting me on."
18. "Psst!"
19. "Stay away from me!"
20. "Who? *Me*?"
21. "C'mon in, the water's fine."
22. "Cluck, cluck. You sound like a bunch of chickens."
23. "I've had it up to here with your nonsense!"
24. "Welcome to our home."
25. "He's a little goofy."
26. "Let me say, first. . ."
27. "Spare a dime, mister?"
28. "Stop right there!"
29. "You *naughty* girl!"
30. "How do you like my hairdo?"

33 Choose one of the topics from the listings below. Then go to the front of the class and talk about the topic "off-the-cuff" for a minute or so. The only rule is this: You must keep both hands behind your back through the whole talk. When you are finished talking, show your classmates some of the gestures you would have used if you had been allowed to.

TOPICS

For the Boys:
1. Describe a three-car auto accident you witnessed at a busy intersection.
2. Describe a beautiful girl in a bikini whom you saw at a swimming pool.
3. Explain the game of soccer, or another sport of your own choice.
4. Describe some person, place, thing, or event assigned to you by the *girls* in the class.

For the Girls:
1. Describe to a hairdresser how you want your hair cut and shaped.
2. Describe a handsome boy whom you saw playing football.
3. Explain knitting.
4. Describe some person, place, thing, or event assigned to you by the *boys* in the class.

34 In a newspaper or magazine, find a recent political speech and pretend that you wrote it. But the speech you wrote (the version that the speaker actually read) is somewhat different from the printed version. The difference is this: your version included *directions* to the speaker, telling him when to gesture with his hands and what gestures to use in each instance. The printed version did not include these directions. Reproduce this original version. Copy a portion of the speech from the newspaper or magazine. Then, using parentheses around your directions, create a copy of the version read by the public official. Bring your completed product to class and exchange it for a speech prepared by one of your classmates. Each member of the class then has five minutes in which to study the speech he has been handed. When the study time is up, each member should be prepared, when called on, to read the speech to the class. Follow all gesture directions precisely during each reading.

A FEW PARTING GESTURES, OR JESTURES, BEFORE MOVING ON.

35 The man in the cartoon demonstrates a variety of postures, or "body English." But his posture in the last frame is quite different from his postures in the earlier frames. Why do you think he changes to an up-straight posture when his son enters the room? Two answers, at least, are possible. One of them is pretty easy to guess, the other not so easy. Discuss both possible answers with your classmates and determine what is being said by the man's postures in frames one to five and then in frame six. Then try some body English of your own. Place two chairs side-by-side at the front of the room. Two volunteers from the class seat themselves in the chairs. Next, as each sentence to the right is read, both volunteers translate the sentence into body English. Assume that both persons are listening to the conversation of a third person. Following each dual translation, discuss with your classmates (1) the differences, if any, between the two translations, and (2) other possible translations which should be demonstrated. The two actors should hold their poses while each discussion is in progress.

TRANSLATE INTO BODY ENGLISH

1. "I'm absolutely fascinated by what you are saying."
2. "What you are saying is in poor taste and embarrasses me."
3. "Talk all you want, but my mind is made up."
4. "I'm open to suggestion."
5. "You're boring me."
6. "What do you mean, saying a thing like that about me?"
7. "Finish what you have to say. I have another appointment."
8. A sentence of your own choice.

JACQUES FAIZANT, FRANCE DIMANCHE, FRANCE

Nonverbal Communication

36 The arm and body postures shown in all four pictures are roughly the same. Yet, two of the pictures show winners and two show losers. What's going on here? Does this mean that in body language, as in spoken language, the same statement can sometimes mean two directly *opposite* things? Or is it possible that the postures shown in the pictures are actually expressions of exactly the *same* meaning, in spite of the clearly different circumstances? What do you think? Can you think of any other circumstances in which this particular body English is commonly employed?

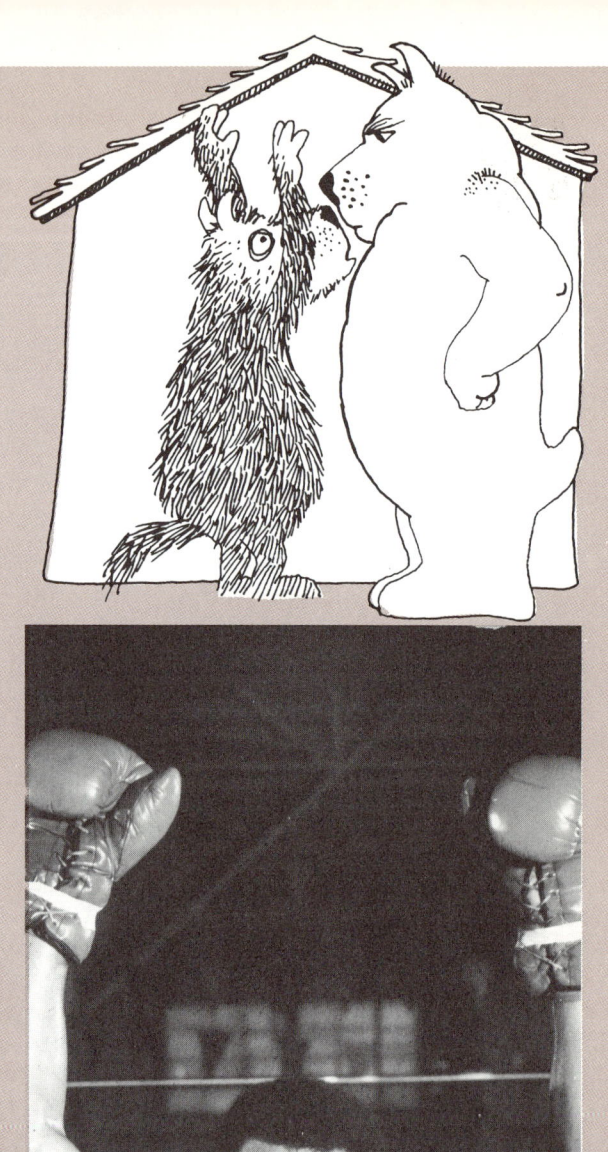

Chain reaction.

37 Discuss the body language of each of the characters in the cartoon below. Which of the two captions do you think is more suitable?

A knowledge of body language is important to a cartoonist. Just how important will be made clear by the following activity. With a classmate, go to the front of the room and present a tableau (no words or motion) that, if photographed or drawn, would be an appropriate cartoon for your choice of one of the captions printed to the right. You and your partner should spend a couple of minutes talking about your roles, planning poses, and so forth, before performing.

CAPTIONS

1. "Don't interrupt me when I'm interrupting you!"
2. "Sometimes I feel as though you're deliberately ignoring me."
3. "Good news, son! I found a college willing to accept you!"
4. "Well, I'm the football coach—and I say that there will be no meetings of Women's Liberation in *my* locker room!"
5. "Doctor, you've got to help me. Everywhere I go, people seem to put me down with body language."
6. A caption of your own choice.

Caption 1: "I wish you'd listen more attentively!"
Caption 2: "You're deliberately paying attention just to confuse me."

Nonverbal Communication

JACQUES FAIZANT, FRANCE DIMANCHE, FRANCE

38 Discuss the body language of the major characters in these two drawings. What is the message of each of the characters? Which characters seem to be fully aware that they are using body language? Which characters are probably using body language without realizing it? Note especially the postures of the woman on the beach. Are they true to life?

39 In his drawings and cartoons, James Thurber made especially good use of body language. Six of Thurber's cartoons are shown here. Refer to the cartoons for clues when discussing the questions that follow.

1. The way a person crosses his legs in any conversational situation tells much about his attitude toward the other person's words or conduct. Crossing the legs *toward* the other person means one thing; crossing them *away from* him means quite another. Look back at the three cartoons in Group A and try to decide what each of these two ways of leg-crossing means in terms of body language.

2. Arms folded on the lap or across the chest make a statement in body language that is quite different from that made by unfolded arms. Look back at the three cartoons in Group B and try to decide the message conveyed by each of these two uses of the arms.

42 Nonverbal Communication

"If you can keep a secret, I'll tell you how my husband died."

"I'd dread falling under your spell, Mr. Pierson."

"In first-aid class today we learned eleven different ways to poison people."

A B

"I wonder what dark flowers grow in the mysterious caverns of your soul."

"I suppose all that you men think about is war."

"He's given up everything for a whole year."

Nonverbal Communication 43

 Look in magazines and newspapers for cartoons or photographs in which the body language of the characters seems to go with what is being said in the caption.

For pictures having no caption, write one yourself. Then, without revealing your own caption, ask two or three of your classmates each to write a caption for your picture. Compare the results. Do all of the captions share roughly the *same* translation of the body language in the picture? Or do the captions suggest that you and your classmates read the same body language in somewhat *different* ways?

 Choose some situation in which body language and spoken language seem to be saying two entirely different things.

Then, either alone or with a classmate, act out the situation for the rest of the class. If you cannot think of such a situation from real life, make one up. Do not be afraid of humor and exaggeration. The important thing is that your gestures, postures, and facial expressions clearly contradict what you are verbally saying.

> DO GESTURES, POSTURE, AND FACIAL EXPRESSION EVER *CONTRADICT* THE SPOKEN WORD?

> HE WHO HAS EYES TO SEE AND EARS TO HEAR MAY CONVINCE HIMSELF THAT NO MORTAL CAN KEEP A SECRET.

"Welcome to the team."

The last time the sound on your television set failed, you probably turned it off and called a repairman. If you did, you missed a good opportunity to study nonverbal communication. If there is a TV set in your classroom, turn it on; then turn the sound down until you can't hear it. Watch the facial expressions and body postures of the actors. How well can you guess the spirit of the conversation on the screen? What types of emotions or attitudes seem to come across best without sound? Which features of body language do people seem to use most often—facial expressions? gestures? body posture?

NOTE: If there is no TV set in your classroom, try these questions as a home assignment. Keep a general record of your observations so that you can discuss the assignment next day with your classmates.

43 As an amateur student of the growing science of body language, you might find it interesting to study the nonverbal behavior of someone you know. Choose someone who is known to the entire class; for example, a classmate of yours, a teacher, or a famous person in politics or show business. Then make up a short pantomime in which you show your classmates the body language you think is characteristic of your subject. The purpose is not to make fun of the subject. (Remember, *you* might be someone else's subject.) Instead, the purpose is to show, as faithfully as possible, the gestures, postures, and facial expressions that best represent the body language of your subject. Highly exaggerated pantomime is not allowed, nor is speech. After your performance, the class should try to guess who your subject is. Then your classmates should discuss how well your performance portrayed the subject's body language. Next, with the rest of the class, try to decide whether the subject's body language helps or hinders his communication.

44 The photo collage shown here illustrates some of the many ways in which gestures communicate messages. Choose one of the kinds of nonverbal communication that you've studied so far and try to make a collage from pictures you find in newspapers and magazines that will illustrate the kinds of messages sent in that way. You might elect a Communications Committee to act as judges to determine which designs most effectively demonstrate the variety of messages that can be sent in one nonverbal manner. Title your collage *The Language of Gesture* (or something similar).

TIME TO PUT *POSTURE* OUT TO PASTURE.

Unit 4

SPACE, DISTANCE, and SILENCE

ASSERTING TERRITORIAL RIGHTS

ADJUSTING DISTANCES

During your day you probably come across many situations in which people (1) assert their rights to certain territory and space, or (2) adjust the distance between themselves and others until the distance feels comfortable and appropriate for the situation. With the help of your classmates, make up a list of examples of each type of situation. The lists to the right will help get you started. See how many other items you can add to them.

NOTE: Save your lists for Activity 49.

1. Dad reserving a special chair for himself at home.

2. Mom not liking anyone to use her desk.

1. Explaining a complicated matter to someone (What distance do you attempt to establish?)

2. Talking to someone about a confidential matter.

"Your cat is entering my sphere of influence!"

Nonverbal Communication

 Write a description of a situation you have experienced that, like the two situations below, shows how people either claim particular territory as their own or adjust their distance from other people to suit a particular communication need. If necessary, invent such a situation. You may find it more fun to write your paper as a news item or as an anecdote, instead of as a straightforward description. But the choice is yours. Read and discuss the papers in class.

Back in the years just before World War II, Charlie Chaplin did a motion picture called *The Great Dictator.* As with all of Chaplin's movies, it was filled with bits of body language, but the most delightful sequence was one that took place in a barber shop.

Chaplin as Hitler and Jack Oakie as Mussolini are shown getting shaves in adjacent chairs. The scene centers around the attempts of each to put himself in a dominant position to the other in order to assert his superior leadership. Trapped within their chairs, lathered and draped, there is only one way to achieve dominance, and that is by controlling the height of the chairs. They can reach down and jack them up. The higher man wins, and the scene revolves around the attempt of each to jack his own chair to a higher position.

from *Body Language*
by Julius Fast

The Korean armistice talks, which have dragged on through 275 sessions, have provided some classic examples of the use of punctilio[1.] to shatter a rival's composure. At one of the first meetings, North Korea's General Nam Il provided himself with a particularly high chair and seated U.S. Admiral C. Turner Joy on a low one. Joy saw to it that the chairs were of equal height from then on. When the allies set out a small United Nations table flag, the North Koreans followed suit—only theirs was six inches taller. In this case, however, Joy "hastened to veto any tendency toward such competition," as he wrote in his book. *How Communists Negotiate*, "thereby perhaps averting construction of the two tallest flagpoles on earth."

from *Time*, December 13, 1968

[1.] *punctillio:* a fine point in observance of ceremony.

 **Part A:** The news report below describes a small, but important, incident. Read the item carefully until you understand the problem in international diplomacy that faced the delegates to the conference. Discuss with your classmates why the seating plan was so important. Then look at the item from *Vogue's Book of Etiquette and Good Manners* in Part B.

THE PARIS CONFERENCE   All Set to Talk - But No Place to Sit

During 7 1/2 hours of private talks in Paris last week, the U.S. and North Viet Nam settled all but two of the procedural problems that have delayed the beginning of an expanded peace conference. They agreed, for example, that the salon of the Hotel Majestic, where the talks on the Viet Nam war have been under way since May, is large enough, after all, to accommodate the expanded talks. They also decided that two doors should be used, one for the representatives of Hanoi and of the National Liberation Front, the other for delegates from Saigon and the U.S.

Unfortunately, the two issues left unresolved were probably the most important of all. One was a date for the first meeting involving all four sides (Secretary of State Dean Rusk predicted that it would be held some time this week.) The other was the shape of the negotiating table. Hanoi wanted a square one, which would give the N.L.F.[1] a side to itself. As the Communists see it, that arrangement would enhance the guerrillas' claim to independent status. The Allies apparently see it the same way. They want two rectangular tables, with the U.S. and South Viet Nam seated at one, and North Viet Nam and the N.L.F. at the other, to prevent the guerrillas from getting a whole side of a table to themselves. It might have seemed absurd, but in the past, conferences on grave issues have foundered over such trivial "modalities."[2] And as Hanoi Spokesman Xuan Thuy noted, "Whether it is important or not, it must be resolved. You cannot sit down at a conference without a table."

from *Time*, December 13, 1968

"Heaven Knows, We've Tried Everything Else"
Distributed by the *Los Angeles Times* SYNDICATE

[1] *The National Liberation Front, or Vietcong, is a guerrilla organization in South Vietnam with whom the North Vietnamese government is allied.*

[2] *modalities: methods of operation*

Nonverbal Communication 49

When there is no host, the woman guest of honor sits to the right of the man at the hostess' right, providing they are not married. If they are, she sits to the left of the man at the hostess' left.

A TABLE FOR TWELVE WITH NO HOST

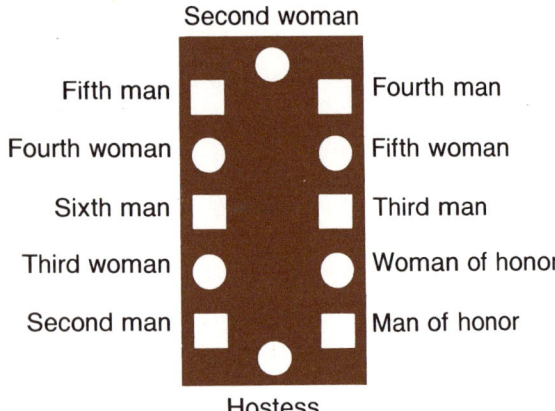

This diagram is correct only if the man and woman guests of honor are not married. Twelve being a multiple of four, a woman faces the hostess at the other end of the table. To avoid this, a dinner without a host must number six, ten, fourteen, or eighteen.

from *Vogue's Book of Etiquette and Good Manners*

Part B: Now that you have thought about some of the more important concerns of international diplomacy and etiquette, you are no doubt ready to write a book on the subject! Well, not really a book. Using the diagram and notes at the left for guidelines, write a one-page paper entitled "Proper Diplomatic Etiquette in the Seating of Delegates to International Conferences" in which you suggest your solution to the problem faced at the Paris Conference. Pay special attention to all matters having to do with the use of space and territory. You might find that writing two sections, one titled *DO* and the other *DON'T*, is the best way to organize your paper. And don't be afraid to use diagrams such as the one to the left. Share your finished paper with your classmates. Discuss with them the various solutions suggested in the papers. Choose the two or three best papers. Then, with class members playing the roles of conference delegates, try the seating arrangements suggested in the papers you chose.

The next four activities use points made in *this part* of a longer article by Edward and Mildred Hall. You may look back at it as often as you want when doing each of the next four activities.

In crowded public places, we tense our muscles and hold ourselves stiff, and thereby communicate to others our desire not to intrude on their space and, above all, not to touch them. We also avoid eye contact, and the total effect is that of someone who has "tuned out." Walking along the street, our bubble expands slightly as we move in a stream of strangers, taking care not to bump into them. In the office, at meetings, in restaurants, our bubble keeps changing as it adjusts to the activity at hand.

Most white middle-class Americans use four main distances in their business and social relations: intimate, personal, social and public. Each of these distances has a near and a far phase and is accompanied by changes in the volume of the voice. Intimate distance varies from direct physical contact with another person to a distance of six to eighteen inches and is used for our most private activities—caressing another person or making love. At this distance, you are overwhelmed by sensory inputs from the other person—heat from the body, tactile stimulation from the skin, the fragrance of perfume, even the sound of breathing—all of which literally envelop you. Even at the far phase, you're still within easy touching distance. In general, the use of intimate distance in public between adults is frowned on. It's also much too close for strangers, except under conditions of extreme crowding.

In the second zone—personal distance—the close phase is one and a half to two and a half feet; it's at this distance that wives usually stand from their husbands in public. If another woman moves into this zone, the wife will most likely be disturbed. The far phase—two and a half to four feet—is the distance used to "keep someone at arm's length" and is the most common spacing used by people in conversation.

The third zone—social distance—is employed during business transactions or exchanges with a clerk or repairman. People who work together tend to use close social distance—four to seven feet. This is also the distance for conversations at social gatherings. To stand at this distance from someone who is seated has a dominating effect (e.g., teacher to pupil, boss to secretary). The far phase of the third zone—seven to twelve feet—is where people stand when someone says, "Stand back so I can look at you." This distance lends a formal tone to business or social discourse. In an executive office, the desk serves to keep people at this distance.

The fourth zone—public distance—is used by teachers in classrooms or speakers at public gatherings. At its farthest phase—25 feet and beyond—it is used for important public figures. Violations of this distance can lead to serious complications. During his 1970 U.S. visit, the president of France, Georges Pompidou, was harassed by

Nonverbal Communication 51

pickets in Chicago, who were permitted to get within touching distance. Since pickets in France are kept behind barricades a block or more away, the president was outraged by this insult to his person, and President Nixon was obliged to communicate his concern as well as offer his personal apologies.

It is interesting to note how American pitchmen and panhandlers exploit the unwritten, unspoken conventions of eye and distance. Both take advantage of the fact that once explicit eye contact is established, it is rude to look away, because to do so means to brusquely dismiss the other person and his needs. Once having caught the eye of his mark, the panhandler then locks on, not letting go until he moves through the public zone, the social zone, the personal zone and, finally, into the intimate sphere, where people are most vulnerable.

from "The Sounds of Silence" by Edward and Mildred Hall

48 In their article, the Halls describe "four main distances" that people use in their daily lives. What is the name given by the Halls to each of the distances? And what specific space, expressed in feet or inches, is assigned to each main distance? Jot down the answers to both questions on a sheet of scrap paper. Note that each main distance (or zone) has a *near phase* and a *far phase*. You will want to jot down the measurement of *both* phases in each of the four main categories. When you have written down these figures, copy them onto a diagram of your own design that shows the distances more or less to scale. One way you might set up your diagram is to draw a series of concentric circles. The center represents a person. The radius of each circle corresponds, in each instance, to one of the distances mentioned by the Halls. Circles showing the outer limits of the *far* phase in each of the four main categories could be drawn in dark lines; circles showing near phases could be drawn in lighter lines. Label your diagram thoroughly. Each main category should be shown with its near and far phases clearly marked in feet or inches. Underneath the finished diagram, list the example situations given by the Halls for each phase of each main category. Keep your diagrams for later use.

 Take out the lists you made under **ADJUSTING DISTANCES** in Activity 45 on page 47. Discuss with your classmates how you would relate each item on the list to one of the main distances or zones shown in your diagram. Be sure to decide, too, which phase, near or far, of the zone more closely suits each situation.

 Do you think that the Halls would think either of the panhandlers in the cartoons is a master at panhandling? Respectable and worthwhile organizations often ask for donations from people in the street. Perhaps you have worked for such an organization. Now pretend that you head up a group of fellow students who want donations to help a local charity. You have decided to have your helpers ask for donations from shoppers on the main street of your town or city. Local authorities have given you a permit to do this. So that your helpers can solicit as much money as possible, write one page of instructions that describes the ways of street soliciting that you feel will be (1) *most* successful, and (2) *least* successful. Two lists, one for *DOs* and one for *DON'Ts*, should be sufficient.

"*A quarter and I'll worship the ground you walk on.*"

Nonverbal Communication

 From a newspaper or magazine, cut out one drawing or photo for the near and far phases of the four main distances mentioned by the Halls. Bring your eight choices to class with you and exchange them for the pictures gathered by another member of your class. Each of you should try to guess which illustration goes with which phase and zone of interaction. When you have made your guesses back and forth, return the pictures to their owner. Then the two of you choose the best group of eight from your sixteen pictures. Keep in mind that you must cover all phases and zones. Label each of the final choices on the back, telling the phase and zone it is supposed to represent. Finally, if no one volunteers, by class vote elect a Master Designer from the class. Give your packet to the student selected. Over a period of days he will construct a large collage of PEOPLE INTERACTION for the class.

 Scientists who study human behavior have found that each of us lives inside a private "bubble" surrounding the territory we wish to protect from invasion by others. The size of the bubble is different for each individual. People who prefer to live in the suburbs, for example, might be said to have larger bubbles—they need a sense of distance between themselves and their neighbors. City dwellers, on the other hand, have smaller bubbles—they can tolerate close neighbors. This sense of private territory is easily observed in the behavior of most animals. Dogs, for example, protect their masters' property from intruders—other animals or people—without being trained to do so. Just as important, other dogs respect a dog's "right" to territory. This sense of private territory, in animals or in man, is always shown in nonverbal ways. Humans do not hang signs on themselves giving the size of their private bubbles. But other people somehow get the message. You might like to discuss with your classmates a few situations in which this idea of territory affects the general behavior of both man and animals. Here are a few topics to help get you started. ☞

1. Crowded areas of cities are often referred to as jungles. This term seems particularly appropriate in view of the teenage gang wars that often plague such areas. Why do you think cities are so violent?

2. How might you account for the popularity of communes?

3. Lion tamers who perform in circus cages have a great deal of courage. However, they have something in addition to courage going for them. They *know* something. What do you suppose this something is?

4. A recent study conducted in several inner-city ghetto areas found that almost everyone living in these areas stood about one foot distant when conversing. Assume that you are an architect. How might you apply the results of this study to your design of a new city housing project for people who now live in ghettos?

5. Two houses having roughly the same number of rooms and other features, but standing on house lots very different in size, are usually widely different in selling price too. Which house usually costs more — the house on a large or small lot? Is this merely a matter of "the more for the money, the more money"? Suppose you were a real-estate salesman in a suburban town with both crowded and uncrowded residential sections. Into which type of section would you take (1) a customer hoping to move to your town from a city ghetto, and (2) a customer from a rural area?

53 Here is an outside activity you might enjoy: Elect a committee to make a study of the zoning laws in your town or your city. (If you live in a large city, study the zoning laws only for the neighborhood in which you live.) You should be able to get copies of the laws at the office of the local planning and zoning board. The laws spell out such things as how much land is required for building a private dwelling and whether dwellings for more than one family are permitted. Study the laws and determine whether the town in which you live is a "big bubble" or a "small bubble" area. Then make an oral report of your findings to the class. Give as much specific evidence as possible.

The distance between a speaker and a listener in any situation depends pretty much on what is being said. For example, if a speaker and listener are holding a secret conversation, they stand very close to each other. The distance becomes greater when the conversation is not so secret. The chart below lists some of the relationships between distance and what is being said. The first item on the chart has been filled in for you. Other items on the chart are complete *except for* the actual distances in each category. Try to complete the chart by filling in all the empty parentheses. Find a tape measure and do some experimenting. Work in groups of three or four. Act out each of the situations and write down the distances that you think apply for each. Bring back your results and compare them with those of the other groups. Did each group arrive at roughly the same average distance in each category? If wide differences in distance are noted, what might have caused them?

1. Very Close (3' - 6') — Soft whisper; top-secret

2. Close ( ) — Audible whisper; very confidential

3. Near ( ) — Indoors, soft voice; outdoors, full voice; confidential

4. Neutral ( ) — Soft voice, low volume; personal subject matter

5. Neutral ( ) — Full voice; information of non-personal matter

6. Public Distance ( ) — Full voice with slight overloudness; public information for others to hear

7. Across the Room ( ) — Loud voice; talking to a group

8. Stretching the Limits ( ) of Distance — Indoors; up to 100 feet outdoors; hailing distance

Nonverbal Communication

 Read both selections on this page. Then discuss with your classmates the topics following the selections.

In Latin America the interaction distance is much less than it is in the United States. Indeed, people cannot talk comfortably with one another unless they are very close to the distance that evokes either sexual or hostile feelings in the North American. The result is that when they move close, we withdraw and back away. As a consequence, they think we are distant and cold, withdrawn and unfriendly. We, on the other hand, are constantly accusing them of breathing down our necks, crowding us, and spraying our faces.

Americans who have spent some time in Latin America without learning these space considerations make other adaptations, like barricading themselves behind their desks, using chairs and typewriter tables to keep the Latin American at what is to us a comfortable distance. The result is that the Latin American may even climb over the obstacles until he has achieved a distance at which he can comfortably talk.

from *The Silent Language*
by Edward T. Hall

I had three chairs in my house; one for solitude, two for friendship, three for society. When visitors came in larger and unexpected numbers there was but the third chair for them all, but they generally economized the room by standing up. It is surprising how many great men and women a small house will contain. . . .

One inconvenience I sometimes experienced in so small a house (was) the difficulty of getting to a sufficient distance from my guest when we began to utter the big thoughts in big words. You want room for your thoughts to get into sailing trim and run a course or two before they make their port. The bullet of your thought must have overcome its lateral and richochet motion and fallen into its last and steady course before it reaches the ear of the hearer, else it may plow out again through the side of his head. Also, our sentences wanted room to unfold and form their columns in the interval. Individuals, like nations, must have suitable broad and natural boundaries, even a considerable neutral ground, between them. . . . As the conversation began to assume a loftier and grander tone, we gradually shoved our chairs further apart till they touched the wall in opposite corners, and then commonly there was not room enough.

from *Walden*
by Henry David Thoreau

58 Nonverbal Communication

1. Suppose that you and your classmates had been able to watch Thoreau and his friends in conversation and had used what you saw as the sole evidence for filling in the chart in Activity 53. What differences, if any, would such a chart have, compared with the chart you completed for that activity?

2. Basing your opinion only on the selection printed here, do you think that Thoreau would have been a good U.S. Ambassador to a Latin American country? Explain your view.

 Choose either Part A or Part B of this activity.

Part A: Write a short paper describing a situation from your own experience in which the distance between you and another person or persons played a large part in a communication failure. Try to describe the failure in terms of the "private bubble" surrounding each party to the incident. Did you need more distance, or less? What would you say you learned from the incident? How do you intend to put that knowledge to good use if a similar situation arises again? Some of the papers should be read by the class.

Part B: If you prefer acting to writing, find a classmate who feels the same way. Prepare a series of quick skits in which you show at least five cases of the wrong use of distance in communication situations. Try to come up with situations not already discussed by the class. Perform the skits for your classmates. At the end of each skit, show the correct use of distance in the situation involved.

IT'S TIME NOW TO MOVE ON TO *SILENCE*, THE LAST NONVERBAL FACTOR YOU'LL BE ROPED INTO STUDYING IN THIS BOOK.

Nonverbal Communication

"You're too sensitive. I detect no air of silent reproach."

Almost everyone, at one time or another, is given the silent treatment by another person. The cartoon describes silence of this sort as an "air of silent reproach." It is important to know the difference between this kind of silence, which substitutes for the words a person could say, and ordinary silence, which occurs when people are simply not talking. Discuss with your classmates situations from your own experience in which you either gave or received the silent treatment. Mention in each description the *words* for which the silent treatment was a substitution. Would communication have been better if the words had been spoken? Or was the message clear enough, even though silent? Write down on a piece of paper any description of a silent treatment—including the "missing" words—that strikes you as especially amusing. Save your notes for the next activity.

60 Nonverbal Communication

 Draw a comic strip (more than one frame) to illustrate the silent treatment situation you wrote down during the previous activity. Introduce the situation in the early frames. Use speech "balloons" in these frames to show conversation between characters. The actual silent treatment occurs in the final frame. In this frame, write the missing words in a "thought" balloon over the head of the character giving the treatment. Don't spend too much time on the art; simple drawings without background will be fine. Display your finished product on the classroom bulletin board under some general label such as "The Power of Silence."

"Hush, my dear! You're contributing to the noise pollution!"

Here are some quotations about silence. Read all the quotations. Then choose one and write a paragraph explaining the meaning of the quotation. Some of the quotations contain words you may not know. Use your dictionary for help in defining these words. When everyone has written his paragraph, some of the papers should be read aloud. Challenge any paper that does not, in your opinion, correctly explain the quotation it is meant to explain.

1. "It takes a man to make a room silent." *Henry David Thoreau*

2. "Silence is the unbearable repartee." *G. K. Chesterton*

3. "Silence is the language of all strong passions: love, anger, surprise, fear." *Giacomo Leopardi*

4. "It is always observable that silence propagates itself, and that the longer talk has been suspended the more difficult it is to find anything to say." *Samuel Johnson*

5. "Silence is not always tact and it is tact that is golden, not silence." *Samuel Butler*

6. "Silence, to a wise man, *is* an answer." *Euripedes*

7. "The Diplomat sits in silence, watching the world with his ears." *Leon Samson*

8. "Silence gives consent." *Oliver Goldsmith*

9. "He who sleeps in continual noise is wakened by silence." *William Dean Howells*

10. "Well-timed silence has more eloquence than speech." *Martin Farquhar Tupper*

Nonverbal Communication

The Unwritten

Inside this pencil
crouch words that have never been written
never been spoken
never been thought

they're hiding

they're awake in there
dark in the dark
hearing us
but they won't come out
not for love not for time not for fire

even when the dark has worn away
they'll still be there
hiding in the air
multitudes in days to come may walk through them
breathe them
be none the wiser

what script can it be
that they won't unroll
in what language
would I recognize it
would I be able to follow it
to make out the real names
of everything

maybe there aren't
many

it could be that there's only one word
and it's all we need
it's here in this pencil

every pencil in the world
is like this   W. S. MERWIN

 Write a poem that follows the ideas in "The Unwritten" by W. S. Merwin. But entitle your own poem: "The Unspoken."

THE NEXT-TO-LAST WORD

 As your final activity in this book, choose either one of the following activities:

1. Draw another diagram of the Communication Circuit similar to the one you drew for Activity 7, page 12. But this time, use only aspects of *nonverbal* communication in the diagram. Display your completed work on the classroom bulletin board.

2. Create a collage entitled "The Complete Guide to Nonverbal Communication." Display your design in the classroom.

One advantage of saying it with flowers is th...

THE LAST WOR

"He's a man of few words."

COSPER, HUDIBRAS, DENMARK